That it might be fulfilled

The Prophecies of Matthew 1 & 2

I0159629

Daniel Andersen

ISBN: 978-1-78364-261-8

www.obt.org.uk

****

The Open Bible Trust
Fordland Mount, Upper Basildon,
Reading, RG8 8LU, UK.

That it might be fulfilled

The Prophecies of Matthew 1 & 2

Contents

*

That it might be fulfilled

That it might be fulfilled

Fill: (from Anglo-Saxon *fyllan*) "To put or pour into, till no more can be received" (Webster's Collegiate Dictionary, first of 11 meanings!).

Fulfill: (from Anglo-Saxon *fulfyllan*) "To carry into effect, as an intention; to bring to pass, as a design; also, reflexively, to realize or manifest completely" (Webster's Collegiate Dictionary).

pleroo: (pronounced "play-rah-o") "to fill, make full, fill up" (Bagster's *Analytical Greek Lexicon,* Thayer's *Greek-English Lexicon.* Both also list several secondary and derived meanings such as "to realize, accomplish, fulfil".)

When we read in the New Testament scriptures of something taking place in order to "fulfil" something from the Old Testament scriptures, the Greek verb *pleroo* is used. Typical of such simple words, it has a basic meaning and a variety of secondary and derived meanings. An example of its use with its basic meaning (as indicated above) is Luke 3:5: "every valley shall be *filled.*" An example of its use with a more extensive meaning is Luke 9:31: "... and spake of his decease which he should *accomplish* at Jerusalem." This latter passage clearly suggests the meaning of bringing to pass or carrying an intention into effect, as indicated for the word "fulfill" above.

We see, then, that the one Greek verb *pleroo* can be used for both the English "fill" and "fulfil". Perhaps there is a thought here worth considering. Our English word "fulfil" lends itself to the ideas of "partial fulfillment", "dual fulfillment", even many "fulfillments", as when an intention is partly realized or realized one or more times. I have heard mention of "partial fulfillment", "dual fulfillment", even "tertiary fulfillment" of scripture prophecies. But I wonder if the Greek verb can lend itself to such usage. I have the feeling that the basic idea of "making full" or "filling up" is implicit in each use of *pleroo*.

So when we read of something being "fulfilled" in the New Testament, it seems to me to indicate that this is the definitive "filling up" in regard to that particular situation. It is neither a "partial fulfilment" awaiting something more complete later on nor the first of a succession of "fulfilments", whether two or three or more. Even in Luke 9:31 we do not lose the thought of something being made full in the realization or accomplishment of a purpose. The *New English Bible* renders this phrase: "the destiny he was to fulfil in Jerusalem". Phillips translates it: "the end he must fulfill in Jerusalem". It was to be a single completely "filled up" accomplishment with no "partial" or "dual" fulfilments.

Let us keep this thought in mind as we examine some of the "fulfilments" in the New Testament scriptures. It may be possible for us to see more than one "fulfilling" for an Old Testament scripture while the Bible itself indicates a single "making full". An example is John 19:36:

These things happened so that the scripture would be fulfilled: "Not one of his bones will be broken…"

This may have most direct reference to the Passover lamb, Exodus 12:46; Numbers 9:12, with an allusion to Psalm 34:20. The idea of not having a bone broken contained in these Old Testament passages was probably "fulfilled" countless times in the sense of the realization of an intention. But it was "filled up" in a definitive manner just once, in the crucifixion of Christ.

Various ways of "Fulfilling"

Various ways of "Fulfilling"?

As we open the pages of the New Testament we cannot help but be impressed by the numbers of references to "fulfilments" ("fill ups") of Old Testament prophets or scriptures that we come across. There are four of them in the first two chapters of Matthew, five in the first four chapters, and 14 (out of 17 occurrences of *pleroo*) in the entire book. Of these, 13 make mention of a prophet or prophets.

There is a tendency on our part to think of a prophecy as a prediction and the fulfilment of a prophecy as the coming to pass as predicted. An example of where this appears to be the case is Matthew 8:17:

> This was to fulfill what was spoken through the prophet Isaiah: "He took up our infirmities and carried our diseases."

The quotation is from Isaiah 53:4. Some of this chapter appears to make predictions, but most of it, as verse 4, appears to describe things that have already taken place. We interpret it as anticipating the Messiah, so we consider it to be describing future events as though they have already been accomplished.

But this manner of prophecy (as prediction) and fulfilment is certainly not always the case. In fact it may be the style of a minority of cases. Consider Matthew 13:35:

> So was fulfilled what was spoken through the prophet: "I will open my mouth in parables, I will utter things hidden since the creation of the world."

This quotes Psalm 78:2. Matthew uses the psalm in such a manner as to convey the impression that Christ is uttering thoughts never before made known. But the psalm, in its own setting, is not predictive in any sense and doesn't describe telling something not known before. It speaks of uttering "dark sayings" (*KJV*) actually known from antiquity. These are things of hidden meaning, enigmas, obscure sayings, perhaps material put in the form of riddles. This psalm is a Maschil (instruction), suggesting material put in a peculiar form for the oral teaching of Israel's history. (The word used in the Greek translation here is the one from which we get our word "problem"!) We read in verses 3-4 that these sayings are:

> what we have heard and known,
>> what our fathers have told us.
> We will not hide them from their children;
>> we will tell the next generation
> the praiseworthy deeds of the LORD,
>> his power, and the wonders he has done.

So Matthew takes a thought from the psalm and alters it to fit the situation he is describing. The psalm speaks of parables that were known but had hidden meaning. Christ speaks in parables that not only had hidden meaning, but had themselves been hidden, had been concealed, and so were not known. Thus, we see that Matthew adapts an idea from the Old Testament and gives it new meaning, meaning not seen in the original. So "fulfilling" can imply the adaptation of an old idea to a new situation, of actually reinterpreting some ancient material in order to make a particular application. And in so doing, the possible meaning of the words used to convey thoughts and meaning is "made full".

What is a Prophet?

What is a Prophet?

Before considering more of the "prophecies" in detail let us be reminded that a prophet is not necessarily one who foretells the future. A "prophecy" is not necessarily a statement predicting something in the future. The word "prophet" is from *pro* (before in time or before in position) and *phemi* (to utter, tell forth). So it is natural to take a "prophet" as one who utters or tells forth something "beforehand", ahead of time.

But a prophet is primarily a spokesman for another, one who figuratively "speaks before" another, most often a deity, who constitutes or appoints that one as a prophet. A prophet or prophetess of God is one who, in some sense, stands before God and speaks the truths God gives him or her to speak. Most of the prophets and prophesying in the Bible are in relation to God, though we sometimes read of false prophets. What is spoken can relate to the past or present or future.

As it has been put, a prophet is a "forth-teller" (for God), not necessarily a "fore-teller". When the

Roman soldiers taunted the blindfolded Christ, they may have taken turns striking Him and then urging Him to "Prophesy unto us, thou Christ, who is he that smote thee?" (Matthew 26:68). This had to do with predicting something in the future. They taunted Him with the idea that if He were indeed the Christ, God's Anointed One, He should have the gift of divination and thus should know which one of the soldiers struck Him in spite of being blindfolded. The status of Abraham and Sarah in the household of Abimelech changed dramatically when it was revealed to Abimelech that Abraham was a prophet, that is, a spokesman for God (see Genesis 20:7). The honourable Abimelech had great respect for such a person.

A specific prediction

A Specific Prediction

The Bible does contain some specific predictions and clear statements of their "coming to pass as predicted" though they are not spoken of as "fulfilments" or as "being fulfilled". Perhaps the best example is that of John the Baptist.

> This is he who was spoken of through the prophet Isaiah: "A voice of one calling in the desert, 'prepare the way for the Lord, make straight paths for him.'" (Matthew 3:3)

The specific prediction is, of course, Isaiah 40:3. Matthew very simply states that John the Baptist "is he who was spoken of". He does not say that what was spoken by Isaiah was "fulfilled" though you and I might refer to the appearance of John the Baptist as "fulfilling" the words of Isaiah.

I personally do not believe that there are many cases of such specific predictions in the Old Testament writings coming to pass in such a direct manner as we see with John the Baptist. I urge the reader to search for examples of this particular kind and see how many can be found.

That it might be fulfilled 24

Out of Egypt Have I Called My Son

Out of Egypt Have I Called My Son

Let us look in some detail at the "fulfilling" spoken of in Matthew 2:14-15. I consider it the simplest and clearest example to indicate for us the manner and nature of many, if not most, scripture "fulfilments".

> So he got up, took the child and his mother during the night and left for Egypt, where he stayed until the death of Herod. And so was fulfilled what the Lord had said through the prophet: "Out of Egypt I called my son."

The words spoken through the prophet are the Hosea 11:1:

> When Israel was a child, I loved him, and out of Egypt I called my son.

We find nothing of a predictive element in this passage in Hosea in its immediate setting. It is, rather, an historical reference. Hosea goes on to portray the LORD (*Yahweh*) lamenting Israel's subsequent (to the exodus from Egypt) turning away from Him and turning to idolatry, a phenomenon of frequent occurrence in the Old Testament writings.

We can be quite certain that in making this historical reference, Hosea had in mind Exodus 4:22:

> Then say to Pharaoh, "This is what the LORD says: Israel is my firstborn son."

But Matthew states that the words from the prophet Hosea are "made full" or "filled up". How can a reference to an historical even be "filled up"? We see that Hosea refers to an historical event that depicts an intimate relationship to God, that of "son". We could say that the passage in Hosea contains two important ideas: (1) that of coming out of Egypt, and (2) that of a relationship to God spoken of as "son". Perhaps what Matthew intends is that these important ideas are completed, are totally "filled up". The meaning, the idea, of God's Son coming out of Egypt is, as we say, "finalized", never to be added to again.

That the people Israel had a unique relationship to God as "son" is clear from Biblical passages in both the Old Testament and New Testament writings. But though this is clearly the case, the number of times it is mentioned is remarkably small. In Roman's 9:3-4, Paul speaks of his brethren, his "kinsmen according to the flesh: who are Israelites; to whom pertaineth the adoption". The Greek work rendered "adoption" is a compound word that literally means, "a placing in the condition of a son".

The passages we have cited from Hosea and Exodus are about the only ones in the entire Old Testament that indicate clearly and simply the position of Israel as a "national son of God". Isaiah 45:11 uses the plural "my sons". Jeremiah 31:9, perhaps using the name "Ephraim" to represent the northern kingdom of Israel, states "Ephraim is my firstborn". Deuteronomy 32:6; Isaiah 63:16; 64:8; Jeremiah 3:19; 31:9; Malachi 2:10, speak of God in relation to Israel as "father" but do not use the term "son". So we must conclude that the concept of Israel as "son of God" is certainly not frequently mentioned or well developed in the Old Testament scriptures. Perhaps we can say it was an idea whose time had not yet come, the idea of "son of God" was simply not "filled up"!

The Son of God

The Son of God

But what a difference in the New Testament scriptures! The relationship of Christ to God as "son" is stated dozens and dozens of times. A whole book was written to make it possible to believe that "Jesus is the Christ, the Son of God." The voice from heaven when Jesus was baptized by John the Baptist announced: "This is my beloved Son", Matthew 3:17. When Jesus confronted the men in His intimate company with the question as to His identity, Peter replied, "Thou art the Christ, the Son of the living God", Matthew 16:16.

The first thing Paul proclaimed in his ministry concerned Jesus, "that he is the Son of God", Acts 9:20. So it is no wonder that Matthew could write so early in his document that the whole idea of someone or some entity in relation to God as 'son" is "made full" or "filled up". The very idea of the place of son, being "son of God", is fulfilled, is genuinely realized in the Person of the Lord Jesus Christ. He is the real, the genuine, the ultimate Son of God. The sonship of a nation, or people, was a type or pattern of a greater Sonship. So, with the infant Jesus safely brought back out of Egypt, the whole thought or idea of God calling His Son out of Egypt is made full.

What it means to "Fulfill"

What it means to "Fulfill"

So we see that to "fulfill" an Old Testament prophecy does not necessarily mean that a prediction "comes to pass" just as predicted. It must rather be the "making full" or "filling up" of a thought or an idea. Matthew reaches back to something spoken by Hosea that contains no hint that the Messiah would be the Son of God and, in fact, has no immediate Messianic quality. What Matthew does is to take the description or account of a situation or event in Old Testament history and reinterpret it in terms of a situation or event in the New Testament. It is my opinion that most of the Old Testament prophecies cited in the New Testament, especially those that speak of something being "fulfilled", are of this "reinterpretive" character.

We cannot here engage in an exhaustive study of the many ways we find the New Testament using or making reference to Old Testament passages. We have discussed two ways in which this is done.

There are certainly more, and perhaps each of those discussed here can be subdivided into further categories. This is a most fascinating study and I urge the reader to undertake it and see what manners or kinds or categories of such usages can be made. In this connection I heartily recommend the study of Appendix 107 in *The Companion Bible* entitled "The Principle Underlying the Quotations from the Old Testament in the New".

Other "Sons of God" as Types

Other "Sons of God" as Types

Before going on to another New Testament "fulfilment" we should point out that Israel as a "national son of God" does not exhaust the Old Testament types or shadows of the concept "son of God". Two individuals, David and Solomon, are presented as having this relationship to God. The Second Psalm has often been referred to as the Psalm of the Coronation of the King, describing the establishment of David as king in Zion. There we read:

> I (David) will declare the decree: the LORD hath said unto me, Thou art my Son; this day have I begotten thee. (Psalm 2:7, *KJV*)

But the second psalm can hardly be limited to David, as we find by reading these passages: Acts 4:25-27; 13:33; Hebrews 1:5; 5:5. Again we see that Christ enters into the role and relationship of "Son" that was presented in a typical form in the person of David. None of the passages cited speak of scriptures being "fulfilled" but I believe we have every right to say that they indicate to us a "fulfilment" in the sense of the realization of an intention. In Acts 13 we have a "fulfilling" of a slightly different kind:

> And we declare unto you glad tidings, how that the promise which was made unto the fathers, God hath fulfilled (an intensified form of *pleroo*) the same unto us their children, in that he hath raised up Jesus again; as it is also written in the second psalm, Thou art my Son, this day have I begotten thee. (Acts 13:32-33), *KJV*)

In 2 Samuel 7:14 the words, "I will be is father, and he shall be my son" clearly apply to Solomon. He will be the successor to David and the one who would have the honour of constructing the first temple in Jerusalem. The words go far beyond describing the father-son relationship between David and Solomon. They are the words of the LORD (*Yahweh*) and describe a relationship with Solomon transcending that between ordinary human beings.

The LORD will be a father to Solomon; Solomon will be His son. But Hebrews 1:5 applies this phrase directly to the Lord Jesus Christ who emerges pre-eminently as Son of God. Again, though the context does not speak of scriptures as being "fulfilled", I think we have the right to consider this as another "fulfilment" or carrying into effect of a divine intention. Once more we see Christ entering into a relationship that was a type or shadow of something to come. A situation having immediate application in its setting in the Old Testament is adapted to a higher and more meaningful situation by the New Testament writer.

The Voice in Ramah

The Voice in Ramah

The thoughts presented above in the reference to Hosea seem to be reinforced by the next "fulfilment", Matthew 2:17, 18:

> Then what was said though the prophet Jeremiah was fulfilled: "A voice is heard in Ramah, weeping and great mourning, Rachel weeping for her children and refusing to be comforted, because they are no more."

Matthew here quotes Jeremiah 31:15. The question now confronting us is whether this is a direct prediction of the "slaughter of the innocents" by Herod recorded in Matthew 2:16 or whether it is rather an adaptation by Matthew of a situation or event in Old Testament history. There is no doubt as to the location of Bethlehem where Herod had all the children from two years of age and under slain. It is five miles south of Jerusalem, the site of the present village of Beit Lahm. But most scholars consider the village of Ramah, spoken of by Jeremiah, to have been about five miles north of Jerusalem. So Jeremiah could hardly have been making a direct prediction of the event that took place centuries later in Bethlehem.

Some have suggested that the Hebrew word for "Ramah" basically means "height or high place". So Jeremiah may have been speaking of a high place or prominence in the vicinity of Bethlehem, perhaps the high ridge just west of the village (See note in *The Companion Bible* on Jeremiah 31:15). We ponder the implications of the name "Rachel". Do either Jeremiah or Matthew use it of a particular woman, whether in Jeremiah's day or at the time of Herod's massacre? Or is it a common woman's name used to simply represent those Hebrew women who mourned and wept? We must also note that the tomb of Rachel, the wife of Jacob (Israel) and mother of Joseph and Benjamin, is generally thought to be located about half a mile north of town of Bethlehem. We must also remember that Ephraim was a son of Joseph. In the context of Jeremiah 31 the name Ephraim is quite prominent, perhaps used to represent the northern kingdom of Israel at that time.

These are all fascinating things to ponder as we seek to draw forth meaning and understanding from the complex intermingling of all these details in the scripture passages being considered. But I must confess that I think Matthew is reinterpreting a situation in the Old Testament writings with respect to the situation in Bethlehem. The Ramah of old is generally thought to be the place where the captives to be taken to Babylon were brought for deportation. In fact, Jeremiah himself was brought there along with other captives for this purpose. But Jeremiah was released and allowed to stay in the land, as he relates in chapter 40.

The weeping of Rachel in 31:15 is not due to a massacre but because of the deportation. Jeremiah promises that the time will come when captives will return to their own land from the land of the enemy (verses 16-17). To make this return "from the land of the enemy" to "come again to their own border" means the resurrection of those infants Herod slaughtered is too great a degree of "spiritualizing" to suit me! Many translators indicate that 31:15-17 constitute a paragraph rather isolated from the immediate context, showing it separated from what goes before and what comes after. There may be some substance for the idea that it belongs between verses 1 and 2 of chapter 40. Either way, it is consistent with the events of Jeremiah's day and has no essential "predictive" content. Matthew takes the idea of Israelite mothers lamenting their lost children and "fills it up" upon the occasion of the massacre by Herod.

Fulfilling the "Virgin Birth" Prediction

Fulfilling the "Virgin Birth" Prediction

The foregoing discussion provides a background against which to examine Matthew 1:22, 23:

> All this took place to fulfill what the Lord had said through the prophet: "The virgin will be with child and will give birth to a son, and they will call him Immanuel" – which means, "God with us."

Here is another "fulfilment" of something spoken by a prophet. Is it the coming to pass of a direct prediction? Or is it a fulfilment by making a reinterpretation? There are many who claim that Isaiah's statement (Isaiah 7:14) is a specific, definitive, unequivocal prediction of the Virgin Mary giving birth to the baby Jesus.[1] After all, she is "the virgin" spoken of by Isaiah. She was a virgin in the full sense of never having had sexual

---

[1] For more on this subject see *The Virgin Birth* by Theo Todman, published by The Open Bible Trust

union with a man. The birth of the baby Jesus was the result of a miraculous conception in her womb, conception by the Holy Spirit of God (Matthew 1:20; Luke 1:35).

It is very upsetting to those who embrace this claim that some translate Isaiah's statement: "Behold a young woman shall conceive and bear a son." I well remember the uproar when the 1952 *Revised Standard Version* was published with this translation. It resulted in literal Bible burnings as an expression of the strong feeling that God's direct statement of the virgin birth of Christ was being compromised. A footnote in that translation suggesting "virgin" as an alternate rendering for "young woman" was not enough to prevent the outpouring of intense criticism.

We must take a careful and detailed look at Isaiah's words. I urge the reader to read the 7th chapter of Isaiah. We include here a brief summary.

Ahaz, king of Judah, was frightened by a conspiratorial alliance between Rezin, the king of

Syria, and Pekah, the king of Israel (Ephraim, the northern kingdom). Isaiah was told to allay Ahaz's fears, to tell him that the conspiracy would come to nothing, that he should place his trust in the Lord God (*Adonai Yahweh*). Ahaz was probably tempted to seek alliance with Egypt or Assyria as a defense against the Israel-Syria confederacy. In fact, Isaiah told Ahaz to ask a sign, any sign, that would indicate he should trust and not fear. But Ahaz refused to ask for a sign. So Isaiah told him that the Lord would give a sign anyway.

In verse 13 Isaiah speaks, "Hear ye now, O house of David". Some see significance in the plural "ye" and title "House of David" as an indication that the "sign" is not limited to Ahaz, but is a continuing prophecy addressed to the entire lineage and family of David. We question whether or not a "continuing prophecy" could be a meaningful "sign" with immediate effect. The change of the personal pronoun from singular to plural throughout the chapter is fascinating: singular in verses 2, 4, 5, 11, 16 and plural in verses 9, 13, 14. It is difficult to know if this has any real significance. Perhaps Ahaz was accompanied by others associated intimately with him in the government of Judah. In verse 2 we read that when news of the conspiracy was told "the house of David" that "*his* heart was moved". This undoubtedly refers to Ahaz alone, not the continuing lineage and family of David.

So in verse 14 we have the sign: "Behold, a virgin shall conceive, and bear a son, and shall call his name Immanuel", *KJV*. Those who have examined the Hebrew text closely and seek to translate in a strictly literal sense generally render the passage somewhat as follows:

> "Behold, the lass (damsel, maid) is pregnant and shall bear a son and she shall call his name Immanuel."

The Hebrew word here translated "lass" and translated "virgin" in the *King James Version* can be examined in all its other occurrences to get some idea of its meaning: Genesis 24:43; Exodus 2:8; Psalm 68:25; Proverbs 30:19; Song of Solomon 1:3; 6:8. We see that it is variously translated as "virgin" or "virgins", "maid", and "damsels" in the *King James Version*. It appears to be one of about half a dozen Hebrew words that are practically synonyms, somewhat like our English words lass, girl, damsel, maid, maiden, virgin. The Hebrew text of this passage appears to indicate that the young maiden who gives birth to the son is already pregnant and also is the one who is to give the baby the name Immanuel. The Greek Old Testament renders this passage (translated to English!) as follows:

> "Behold, the virgin shall conceive in the womb, and shall bring forth a son, and thou shalt call his name Emmanuel."

This appears to put the pregnancy in the future and to instruct Ahaz to give the name to the baby. The quotation in Matthew 1:23 appears to follow the Greek translation more closely than the Hebrew. Most quotations of the Old Testament found in the New Testament are from the Greek translation of the Old Testament writings. But notice that, in the Greek version, where Isaiah states "*thou* shalt call his name", Matthew states "*they* will call him".

The Sign – Assurance of Ahaz

The Sign – Assurance for Ahaz

The sense of verses 15, 16 may be somewhat as follows (my translation and paraphrasing):

> When the infant learns to distinguish good food from bad food it shall eat curds and honey, but before the boy knows good food from bad food (therefore in the very near future!) the land (of the confederacy) before whose two kings you feel a sickening dread shall be forsaken.

The last phrase is admittedly difficult, but the kings must be Rezin and Pekah, so these verses show an immediate application of the sign, and verse 14 cannot be isolated from them. In fact, verse 17 continues the passage, making the doomed conspiracy of Rezin and Pekah fade into insignificance. Assyria and Egypt loom large in the future and will be of far greater impact.

The following chapters continue to deal with the future role of Assyria. But God wishes His people to know that He is with them and that they should rely on Him rather than seek alliance with any of these powers for protective purposes. This is the implication of the name "Immanuel": "God with us", or "God is with us". It is repeated in verses 8, 10 of chapter 8. This name does not carry the implication that the infant itself is "God, with us". It rather implies that the infant is a token or evidence of God being with His people to undertake for them and to bless them. Countless people have named a son "Immanuel" or "Emmanuel" or the shortened form "Manuel" with no thought that the baby itself is actually God. They look upon the baby as a blessing from God, as evidence or an expression of God being with them to bless them.

Verse 14 seems to indicate that the young maid who was pregnant was clearly known to Ahaz. The identity of the woman and the child has caused much speculation. It might have been another child of Isaiah himself, later than the son spoken of in 7:3. Isaiah plainly states that he and the children given him by the Lord are "for signs and for wonders in Israel from the LORD of hosts", 8:18.

We include here the translation of Isaiah 7:10-14 in the version called *The Living Bible*, a version that paraphrases liberally:

> Not long after this, the Lord sent this further message to King Ahaz: "Ask me for a sign, Ahaz, to prove that I will indeed crush your enemies as I have said. Ask anything you like, in heaven or on earth." But the king refused. "No", he said, "I'll not bother the Lord with anything like that." Then Isaiah said, "O House of David, you aren't satisfied to exhaust my patience; you exhaust the Lord's as well! All right then, the Lord himself will choose the sign – a child shall be born to a virgin! And she shall call him Immanuel (meaning, "God is with us")".

We quote here a footnote in this version at the word "virgin" in verse 14:

The controversial Hebrew word used here sometimes means "virgin" and sometimes "young woman." Its immediate use here refers to Isaiah's young wife and her newborn son (Isaiah 8:1-4). This, of course, was not a virgin birth. God's sign was that before this child was old enough to talk (8:4) the two invading kings would be destroyed. However, the Gospel of Matthew (1:23) tells us that there was a further fulfillment of this prophecy, in that a virgin (Mary) conceived and bore a son, Immanuel, the Christ. We have therefore properly used this higher meaning, "virgin", in verse 14, as otherwise the Matthew account loses its significance.

We see then that by keeping verse 14 in its context, the words of Isaiah have an immediate application. The sign was for that people at that time. I'm sure that if we have been present and heard the dialogue between King Ahaz and the prophet Isaiah, we would have understood Isaiah to be speaking of the situation of that day, of Ahaz's fear of the confederacy between Rezin and Pekah.

This is not to say the passage has no greater meaning. The treatment by Matthew shows that it does. It is by hindsight that we can see more in the passage than we could possibly have seen if we had been there at that time. Because of the birth and ministry of our Lord Jesus Christ, we can go back to entire sections, as chapters 6 through 9 of Isaiah, and connect what would at first appear to be totally disparate thoughts into a unity that centres upon Himself. This seems to me to be the meaning of "that it might be fulfilled". A fulness of meaning not possible at the immediate time becomes evident later on. In fact, the possible meaning and significance is totally "filled up".

Confronting the Issues

Confronting the Issues

Having seen over many years how people react to the differing interpretations of the Isaiah 7 passage, I urge each one to think through the implications of two crucial assumptions:

Assumption 1: The "sign" of 7:14 was to have had immediate impact; a virgin birth seven centuries in the future could not be a sign to Ahaz of the impending collapse of a conspiracy.

Implications: The "virgin" must have been a maiden known to Ahaz and could not have been a virgin in the sense of not having sexual relations with a man. Will any claim there was a miraculous "virgin birth" back in Isaiah's day?!

Assumption 2: The word "virgin" as used by Isaiah in 7:14 must be taken in full technical sense of a woman who has not had sexual relations with a man, that the birth spoken of is to be understood as a truly miraculous "virgin birth".

Implications: This is not, then, a sign applicable to that time and verse 14 has no intimate connection with its context. Further, this statement by Isaiah would have been instantly recognized as the most unusual prediction in the entire Old Testament. It would have been the focus of extreme interest and attention by every Israelite who heard it or read it. It would have drawn forth the fascination and wonder and questioning of multitudes of inquirers, learned and unlearned, of many lands. But we are not aware of any such unusual attention having been given to it.

Israel's Messianic Expectation

Israel's Messianic Expectation

This discussion leads us to make further inquiry. What was the expectation in Israel, in Israelitish thinking, as to the appearing of the Messiah? It is agreed that among Israelites in general there was the expectation of an Anointed One, the Messiah, who would bring God's blessings of liberty, peace, light, truth, and prosperity to that people. How was the Messiah to come? Would he simply appear among them? Or would he be born as ordinary humans are born? Or would he be conceived in a miraculous way? Would he be the product of a "virgin birth"? Was there a tradition built up in Israelitish thought that the Messiah would come as the result of a "virgin birth"? If they did not interpret Isaiah 7:14 as "Messianic", or that it describes a miraculous conception, then what did they expect concerning the Messiah?

To answer these questions we must consult the work of scholars of history, specifically the history of Israelitish thought and the thoughts of early leaders of what we call the Christian Church. I shall refer here to *The Philosophy of the Church Fathers*, by H. A. Wolfson, giving page numbers to certain select quotes from the volume on Faith, Trinity, Incarnation. Concerning the birth of the Messiah, Wolfson makes these emphatic statements:

> With regard to the Messiah, there is not a single passage in the post-Biblical Jewish literature of the time (of the Greek and Roman worlds) in which the Messiah is spoken of as being born without human paternity. (page 171)

> Nor is there any reference to the miraculous birth of the Messiah in the Apocalyptic literature. In Section 4 of the Book of Enoch, in which there is no specific mention of a preexistent Messiah, the Messiah is spoken of simply as being "born." (page 172)

The Hebrew Scriptures were translated into Greek by Jewish scholars in Alexandria, Egypt, in the 3rd century B.C. They used the Greek word *parthenos* in Isaiah 7:14 to describe the young maiden spoken of there.

This is the word used in Matthew 1:23 to describe the "virgin birth" of Christ. Because of this, some might claim that the Jewish translators of the Greek, the so-called *Septuagint Version*, interpreted Isaiah 7:14 as referring to the Messiah and that they had in mind a miraculous conception. Wolfson deals with this possibility:

> Nor is there any evidence of a belief in the supernatural birth of the Messiah among Alexandrian Jews to be found in the *Septuagint* use of the term *parthenon* as a translation of the Hebrew '*almah* in Isaiah 7:14, for there is internal evidence that the *Septuagint* uses this term in the general sense of the Hebrew term *na'arah* in a context where the *na'arah* in question was not a virgin. Cf. Genesis 34:3. (Page 173)

Wolfson's point is that in Genesis 34:3 the Greek translation uses the word *parthenos* twice in speaking of Dinah, who had been "defiled" or "humbled" by Shechem the son of Hamor the Hivite. Thus this Greek word does not necessarily carry the implications conveyed by our idea of true "virginity". Further, the *Greek Analytical Lexicon* (Bagster) states that *parthenos* means "virgin" or "maid". *Strong's Concordance* states that it means "a maiden", and by implication an unmarried daughter.

Wolfson's comments are likely typical of the results of all inquiry into Israelitish thought concerning both the interpretation of Isaiah 7:14 and the birth of the Messiah. The Isaiah passage was not considered to be "Messianic" and there was no expectation that the birth of the Messiah would be by a miraculous conception. These considerations support the idea mentioned earlier that the "fulfilment" spoken of in Matthew 1:22-23 is by an adaptation of an earlier situation or circumstance and reinterpreting it to give the definitive "filling up" of a thought or idea. If the ultimate appearance of the Messiah was so different than the expectation in Israel, if there was no thought or idea or tradition that the Messiah would come by means of a virgin birth, then the simple, straightforward, unadorned accounts in Matthew and Luke burst like a bombshell into history as the writings of the New Testament unfold!

The Acceptable Year

–

The Day of Vengeance

The Acceptable Year – The Day of Vengeance

We conclude this study by considering one of the most fascinating "fulfillments" in the entire Bible.

> The scroll of the prophet Isaiah was handed to him. Unrolling it, he found the place where it is written: "The Spirit of the Lord is on me, because he has anointed me to preach good news to the poor, He has sent me to proclaim freedom for the prisoners and recovery of sight for the blind, to release the oppressed, to proclaim the year of the Lord's favour." Then he rolled up the scroll, gave it back to the attendant and sat down. The eyes of everyone in the synagogue were fastened on him, and he began by saying to them "Today this scripture is fulfilled in your hearing." (Luke 4:17-21)

Our Lord read from Isaiah 61:1-2. But verse 2 in its entirety reads:

> To proclaim the year of the Lord's favour
> and the day of vengeance of our God,
> to comfort all who mourn...

There must be significance in Christ not reading all of verse 2 but stopping at the end of the line speaking of the year of the Lord's favour, or, as the *King James Version* puts it, "the acceptable year of the Lord."

To many this is perhaps the prime example of what is called "rightly dividing the word of truth". Christ made a "division" right in the middle of a verse from Isaiah between a time of God's favour and a time of vengeance. He indicated that the time of His ministry was the time of God's favour, of bringing to pass the beautiful thoughts that went before: good news to the poor, freedom for the prisoners, sight for the blind, release for the oppressed. Here He stops short. For the day of vengeance must be totally different in character. It must be reserved for a totally different time, a day of God's wrath against the iniquity of man.

But this interpretation overlooks the form of poetical structure found in this portion of Isaiah. One common form of Hebrew poetry (there are several) is the rhyme of ideas rather than words. The same basic idea or a similar idea or a parallel idea is repeated in different words. Innumerable examples of this can be found throughout the Old Testament. The Psalms are saturated with them. So are many of the prophets. Here is Psalm 5:1:

> Give ear to my words, o Lord,
> consider my sighing.

And here is Isaiah 53:2:

> He grew up before him like a tender shoot,
> and like a root out of dry ground.

The *King James Version* fails to show poetical structure but most newer translations do display it. To notice and follow such structure makes the reading ever so much more appealing. Read Psalm 16, where this particular form is used throughout!

It is my conviction that Isaiah uses this poetical form frequently in his writings. The implication is that in 61:2 the "year of the Lord's favour" is really the same as the "day of vengeance of our God." But isn't this impossible? How can the long period of a year be the same as or parallel to the short span of a day? How can something spoken of as the LORD'S favour be the same or parallel to what is described as God's vengeance?

Let's do some investigating to find answers to these two questions. It is pleasant to note that favour is associated with a year while vengeance is associated with but a day. But to claim that Isaiah intended this as a *contrast* can be debated. I don't think the "year" and the "day" indicate the length of time something takes place. When one speaks of "the year of one's birth" or "the day of one's birth", one is telling *when* something happened, not *how long* the process took! So the year and the day of Isaiah 61:2 are not in contrast.

They simply tell of the time these things take place. We have a similar pattern in Isaiah 49:8:

> This is what the LORD says:
> "In *the time* of my favour I will answer you,
> and in *the day* of salvation I will help you."

Both phrases simply speak of the time God's blessing and deliverance take place. We must go on to note that Paul quotes this passage in 2 Corinthians 6:2, applying the thought of God's favour (or "time accepted" *KJV*) and salvation to his ministry of Christ.

To answer the second question let us examine Isaiah 34:8 and 63:4 where the rhyme of ideas is found. Here is 34:8:

> For the LORD has a day of vengeance,
> a year of retribution, to uphold Zion's cause.

And here is 63:4:

> For the day of vengeance was in my heart,

and the year of my redemption has
come.

The meaning of this vengeance is made clear in
several places in Isaiah's writing. Note 35:4:

> say to those with fearful hearts,
>> "Be strong, do not fear;
> your God will come,
>> he will come with vengeance;
> with divine retribution
>> he will come to save you."

The entire 35th chapter, especially verses 5-6, have
the same thoughts of blessing, healing, help, and
rejoicing found in 61:1-3. We see then that it is a
time of favour for Israel when God takes
vengeance upon her enemies. Israel is blessed,
restored, liberated, released from bondage when
God deals with those who took her captive and
enslaved her. That is the thought in these three
passages in Isaiah, that speak of vengeance in the
same passage alongside favour and redemption.

Notice how the parallelism and the thoughts of blessings and comfort for God's people continue immediately after the phrases we have been examining in Isaiah 61:2.

> to proclaim the year of the LORD'S favour
>> and the day of vengeance of our God,
> to comfort all who mourn,
>> and provide for those who grieve in Zion –
> to bestow on them a crown of beauty
>> instead of ashes,
> the oil of gladness
>> instead of mourning,
> and a garment of praise
>> instead of a spirit of despair.

These are beautiful thoughts, full of hope and encouragement replacing grief and despair. But Christ gave new meaning to these thoughts and blessings, a new meaning to Israel's old expectations. However, as a prelude to His ministry and to all that would be developed in the New Testament events and history, Christ can only speak of blessing and favour, of what is "acceptable", not of vengeance. He came to save, to bless the world, not to judge it. He came with blessing and redemption in His heart, not the blessing of some by exacting vengeance upon others. So he gives a new meaning, a new interpretation to these beautiful words.

He applies them to His own ministry and work in behalf of the lost sheep of the house of Israel and ultimately in behalf of humanity. Isaiah spoke of the blessings for his people when freed from the tyranny of the enslaving Babylonian Empire. Christ applies those beautiful thoughts to the blessings of being freed from the dominion and power of sin, being released from the shackles of religious tyranny, being delivered from the blindness of mental darkness, ignorance, and superstition. He applies Isaiah's words to the light assurance, and joy that He Himself can give to any who will come to Him in faith. And, in keeping with the thoughts presented in this study, He "makes full", He "fills up" once and for all the wonderful meanings to be given to the words of old.

The reader is urged to continue this study and expand it. We should investigate each passage where a "fulfilling" is mentioned. But we should also examine all the various manners in which the New Testament makes use of material from the Old Testament. It may not always accord with our preconceptions but we should not fear becoming familiar with the ways in which this is done and building our understanding accordingly. To me, such a study reinforces the little saying I learned in childhood:

> The New is in the Old concealed,
> The old is by the New revealed.

As the light of the truths revealed in the New Testament illuminates the thoughts of the Old Testament we are privileged to "behold wondrous things out of thy law", not only in types, shadows, and symbols, but in a variety of historical settings and utterances of the prophets of old. And light will be shed upon our footsteps as we pursue the path of the truth.

About the Author

Daniel Andersen was born in Berlin, New Jersey, USA in 1925 and raised in Jamestown, New York. He studied at Harvard University, Union College, Dallas Seminary, Houghton College, Columbia University and Michigan State University. He was a Professor of Physics at Grand Valley State University and lived with his wife near Grand Rapids, Michigan, USA.

Books by Daniel Andersen

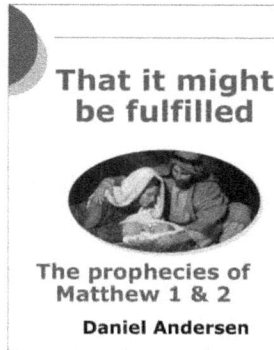

Be Likeminded

one to another

Daniel Andersen

Be reconciled to God

A perspective on biblical evangelism

Daniel Andersen

Bible Study

A personal quest

Daniel Andersen

That it might be fulfilled

The prophecies of Matthew 1 & 2

Daniel Andersen

For details of the above please visit www.obt.org.uk

They can be ordered from that website.

They are available as eBooks from Amazon and Apple and as KDP paperback from Amazon.

Free Magazine

More on Prophecy

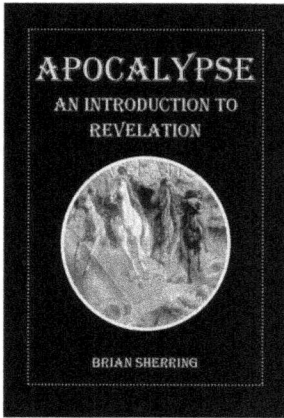

APOCALYPSE
AN INTRODUCTION TO REVELATION

BRIAN SHERRING

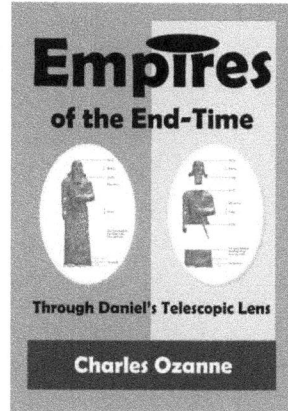

Empires
of the End-Time

Through Daniel's Telescopic Lens

Charles Ozanne

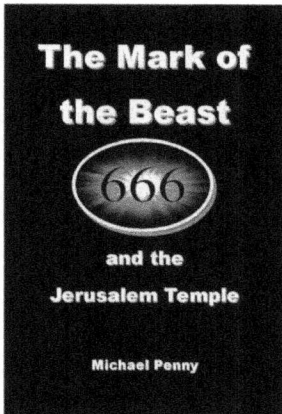

The Mark of the Beast

666

and the Jerusalem Temple

Michael Penny

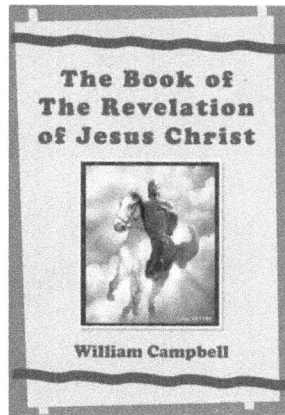

The Book of The Revelation of Jesus Christ

William Campbell

For details of the above please visit
www.obt.org.uk

They can be ordered from that website.

They are available as eBooks from Amazon and Apple and as KDP paperback from Amazon.

About this Book

That it might be fulfilled
The prophecies of Matthew 1 & 2

Often we read in the New Testament scriptures of something taking place in order to "fulfil" something from the Old Testament scriptures. Our English word "fulfil" lends itself to the ideas of "partial fulfilment" or "dual fulfilment" or even "many fulfillments".

The author questions whether the Greek verb can lend itself to such usage. He suggest that when we read of something being "fulfilled" in the New Testament, it means that a "fuller" meaning has been given to the Old Testament passage, that there is "filling up" with regard to that particular passage. It is something being made "full" in realization or accomplishment of a purpose.

Publications of The Open Bible Trust must be in accordance with its evangelical, fundamental and dispensational basis. However, beyond this minimum, writers are free to express whatever beliefs they may have as their own understanding, provided that the aim in so doing is to further the object of The Open Bible Trust. A copy of the doctrinal basis is available at

www.obt.org.uk/doctrinal-basis

or from:

THE OPEN BIBLE TRUST
Fordland Mount, Upper Basildon,
Reading, RG8 8LU, UK.

www.ingramcontent.com/pod-product-compliance
Lightning Source LLC
Chambersburg PA
CBHW070552030426
42337CB00016B/2466